Nearly the *H*appy Hour

Nearly the *H*appy Hour

D. A. PRINCE

To Dick,
with thanks for
such a warm
welcome.
Davina Prince
13 April 2010

HappenStance

First published in 2008
by HappenStance Press
21 Hatton Green
Glenrothes
Fife KY7 4SD
www.happenstancepress.com

Printed by Levenmouth Printers, Buckhaven, Leven KY8 1JH

Typesetting and design by Gerry Cambridge
www.gerrycambridge.com
Set in Baskerville 11.5 / 14

❦

British Library Cataloguing in Publication Data:
A catalogue record for this book is available from the British Library.

ISBN 978-1-905939-07-7

ACKNOWLEDGEMENTS

Thanks to editors of the following magazines in which these poems, or versions of them, previously appeared: *Coffee House*, *Equinox*, *Quattrocento*, *Magma*, *Orbis*, *Other Poetry*, *Pennine Platform*, *Poetry News* (Newsletter of the Poetry Society), *Poetry Nottingham*, *Seam*, *Smiths Knoll*, *South*, *Staple*.

'Handkerchiefs' was runner-up in the Ware Poetry Competition 2002
'Swans' was runner-up in the York Poetry Competition 2003
'Cormorants' was runner-up in BBC Wildlife Competition 2004

Some of the poems, or earlier versions, also appeared in the following pamphlets:

Undoing Time, Pikestaff, 1998
Without Boundaries, Manifold, 2001
Keeping in Touch, Pikestaff, 2002

CONTENTS

11 Writing Just About Parsley
12 That was when
13 And Here's the Proof
14 The Pig-Killing Knife
15 Hearth
16 Kindling
17 *Everything Within*
18 The Long Question
19 String
20 Solomon Grundy
22 School Books
23 Water
24 Sparrows
25 School Photograph: 1957
26 Self-Portrait: With Camera
27 Red Interior: Still Life on a Blue Table
28 What Time is it, Mr Wolf?
29 If the Paper Bag can Learn to Fly
30 Spring
31 Blackbird
32 Not Even in Colour
33 Black Swans, Mating
34 Marriage Bed
35 Familiars
36 Muse
37 *Clever Ways to Create a Clutter-Free Spacious Home*
38 The Day after Valentine's Day
39 Nearly the Happy Hour

40 | Morning Milk
41 | Owls
42 | Late Valencias
43 | This house
44 | Hugo
45 | Cormorants
46 | Attachments
47 | Hope
48 | Swans
50 | Calling Up
51 | Keeping in Touch
52 | Seen from the Train
53 | Red
54 | Taking the Photo
55 | Cooking on the Car Radio
56 | Gull
57 | Undoing Time
58 | Shoes
59 | Sleep
60 | Handkerchiefs
61 | Late October
62 | Absence
63 | Windfalls
64 | Spice Jars
65 | Coats
66 | White Out
67 | Winter Habits
68 | Prospect
69 | High Flight
70 | The Going-Away Dress
71 | One Last Thing
72 | The Other Side

To David

Writing Just About Parsley

An east window and midsummer sun spilling
across the sill and gawky parsley with its trail of stems,
faintness under green translucence.
But so much irrelevance: the kitchen

written over with kettle flex, coffee stains,
skirting boards scrawled with neglect;
light making its own business, cutting new shadows
around teapot, toaster, bread bin, the clutter

of what should be cupboarded—yellowed Pyrex,
a jug from the awkward top shelf;
the window itself, replacing
earlier replacements, and double-locked; how

it draws the parsley close to the glass, facing
the impossible tangle of the garden;
even the silence pleading under its breath,
the radio on standby, humming in time

to the clock—clocks—hidden plumbing,
a settling of bubbles in the drain.
No nearer truth, the barely leaves are tasting
light, first time afloat.

7.30 a.m., the 21st of June.
This year it's flat-leaf; you need to know that.

That was when

all the house-width gardens
had fences—a warped post, the skinniest
ribs you could imagine—and never a hedge
sucking water from
cabbages, potatoes, onions, beetroot,
carrots, swedes, bean rows, the rhubarb

so you looked across the straight and narrow
neighbours' community of weed-free
well-drilled plots, where fathers
worked till supper and at weekends
with their fathers' tools, to nothing that
was any different, except
my mother's lupins, their muddled palette
of knitting-wool colours doing something
unexpected, coarse, and (although
we didn't have the language for it then)
sexual in their thrusting vigour

only we never knew any of that
until disease and age and beetle
levelled them, leaving a soil so poor
it wouldn't even grow weeds.

And Here's the Proof

This one's me, out there, alone,
still remembering how that crimson trike cornered,
brake handles thin as skewers, thumb-heavy bell,
going like the clappers. Hair straight parted,
                              and the middle
bunched up in a bow. Sometimes I see girls
mothered along suburban streets, hair like that,
but never such partings. Front garden, geometry
before the syllabus got there, cut-glass respectable;
a decent rectangle (martyr to moss) and mean border
of meaner roses bullied by blackspot.
Two lanky lilacs and their truant suckers.

So here I am, caught in flight.
Can't see my legs, but they're pumping, stand-up
feet crushed on two pedals; white knuckle grip,
spine in speeding twist and my face screwed
halfway to temper. The words still taste of sour medicine
snapped to camera: *I don't want*
my photo taken.

The Pig-Killing Knife

Growing up with the knife, knowing it
heavy-familiar in the kitchen drawer,
knowing its profile dished where steels had bit,
knowing the annual end it was sharpened for

made all easy as bacon. The blade, quick
and silent, riveted into the vice
of black-blood handles, the neck bully-thick
for speed, saving on pain: it was the price

of food, a working friend. So, nameless pigs
snouting for scraps in cautious nakedness,
calamine-pink, soft as September figs,
met at its point their winter end, the mess

minimal, blood being food. This was life
and getting on with it, no squeamish fear;
and knowing it, growing up with the knife,
has made stabs at tough answers easier.

The pigs were indistinguishable. One
per year, the ham consistently good and sweet,
nothing for nightmares, while the knife lives on
shaped for the hand.

Hearth

My mother had the trick of it
holding a broadsheet page (*The Cambrian News*)
against the leaded grate. She made it fit
tight on the hood, stretched above sullen coals,
kneeling, her fingers fanned out, pulling taut
the paper's risk. Behind the melting print
we'd hear that first shy crack as kindling caught,
then flickered louder. Still she knelt
holding the glow, hiding the heat until
just as the newsprint scorched, she pulled it back.

A solid flame roared up. The chimney gulped.
The coals sang in their scarlet surplices.
A stubby poker gleamed.
Then the browned page
biscuit-crisp and folded, tucked by the fender
for tomorrow's turn. *Don't touch*, she warned,
growing the fire to draw us closer in.

Kindling

He's sawing sideways, awkward,
his mate's thumb too close
to the itchy scratch where bent teeth
stutter into the chipboard.
From a distance it looks like carelessness

cutting to the scene when
I'm locking up our old house for the last time
and there's the new neighbour, nameless,
her bare feet slanted blue as her bedroom slippers,
bracing some scraps of 2x2 on her doorstep
sawing kindling. It's a skill
she's never learned. Frost glints the fence,
and the blade slips and skids, looking
for softer flesh to bite. The scream
when the saw hits stone
lifts starlings from chimney stacks.

Perhaps at last she willed it into sticks,
enough for a first fire, with yesterday's paper crackling,
the kettle on, and eggs frying,
singing to squabbling children.

Behind my back, today's man
is still cutting his inch of broken splinter,
flicking sawdust over his mate's boots.
Fingers crossed.

Everything Within

We grew up believing in its four-inch thick
blue compendium of answers, indexed
under 'Thrifty Home Management',
'An ABC of Wireless'.

There was a 'Dictionary', a 'Gazetteer of the World',
and it fell open at 'Social Letters'—third person
acceptances to third person invitations.

Sunday afternoons taught how it was all done—
complaints to neighbours, or enclosing donations,
all signed Ethel, or Walter, or Cynthia.

Proposals of marriage promising so much. Condolences.
Even then I wondered about death, and how
every letter would tiptoe in the same words.

Its cracked spine was mended, mended, mended.
Changes of address where the ink started
to leak confidence,
and one, two pages coming adrift, misplaced.

With everything within, it needed no company,
was self-sufficient, so the bookcase lodged
boxes of photographs, the iron. Even shoes.

The Long Question

Or I could just go round,
decide whether they use the front door
or the back, and knock—or ring,
they could have bought a bell—
and ask outright, straight up

whether they still use that same leaning post,
grey and runnelled, with its nail for bird bits
and a weathered half-coconut,
even though it was too close to the garage,
had always been, so only ever carried
tea-towels, knickers, vague ragged cloths,
and the sheets had to go further down
sailing over daffodils or lupins or roses in season,
like all the silvery photographs where
I'm playing on the lawn, on a rug

or whether, like everyone else,
they hang their scarcely-dirty washing
on a web of plastic wires, leaving
the posts to rot, or fall, or hack
each one for the bonfire, the clearing out.

String

Ours was passed round the family on parcels,
and never cut, only teased
out of its obstinate knots—one good reason
to stop biting your nails.

It kept well in a dresser jug—door end,
by the garage key with its bent metal tag;
coiled, the end rolled, tucked in, made fast
in ways you picked up
without thinking.

Like so much:
brown paper (flattened under a cushion);
stamp edging (hoarded in a purse);
paperclips (shining in a toffee tin).
All the things you couldn't buy,
even if you'd thought of it.

I never knew you could buy string.

Solomon Grundy

We knew him as one of the family—
like Tom, Tom the Piper's son, or Mr March
the landlord with his Gallagher's tins
for doll's-house tables, or the man
with nerves who tuned the piano.

Give me a name and I'll spill their histories
like coal sacks up-ended in the rattling bunker,
and how they fitted in snug—
sisters, brothers lying like bricks in the local bond,
and every slate roof pitched over mother, father—
and whether they had cats or a dog.

Born on a Monday, with the washing;
christened on Tuesday (piano lessons);
married on Wednesday (half-day closing)
and after that, blanketed
in the ritual hush as women whisper—
ill, worse, died. Buried.

Spooned into us with syrup of figs, and Virol,
he was nothing special: one of us. How
he got into a nursery rhyme we never asked;
everyone knew him like the pencilled dates
in the family Bible.

But nobody noticed
when he slid from memory and out
from the gaudy pages of sing-along rhymes
into the half-remembered roll-call
of second cousins. Missing

from parish registers, not caught by the census,
he never made it to *In Loving Memory*.
Now he's only a smudge in the margin
or, on a good day,
a footnote in the smallest print of all.

School Books

She tucked each corner tight
as a hospital bed, the crackle
of brown paper tracked
into thick folds, each spine
packed with a pleat.
All the geometric precision of tea-tables well set,
knives set-squared, teaspoons drawn
at forty-five degrees in saucers.
She black-lettered each title, loving the promise
of heavy-weight serious words;
underlined family name, and annual
hitch up the school ladder.

Saw them jammed into satchels,
rubbing up against leather journeys,
thumped in saddlebags. Watched them change
with familiarity, grow stranger
with distances travelled, blurring
edges of known, and not-known;
growing, grown.

Water

runs in the family, my father says
plumbing the rough hedge, deep
in hawthorn, bramble, till his hands
recognise the fit of hazel. One slice
with the knife I'm never allowed to touch
and it's sprung, his trap
for mapping springs, and their secret
underground channellings.

He picked it up,
its twisted fluent tongue,
easy as speech, quick as his father's trade.
Born to bricks, he took for granted
native bonds, their strength in walls or wells,
and skills like mixing mortar, levelling,
and sealing off; and likewise
how the hazel dipped and reared,
compelled by liquid signals,
codes of water, translated
down Plynlimon's torrents and sour rushes,
slipping into thin soil through shale.
Perhaps the day he learned was like today:
late May, young lambs now clever with grass,
blackbirds as sharp as slate
scoring their songs on the blue air.

Walking this stubborn field,
stumbling, my hands closed within his, pulse to pulse,
I feel the hazel buck and curve, watch
in wonder the wrenching message as it tracks
the clean lie of water.

Sparrows

So common we ignored them: everywhere,
taking for granted their permanence—gutters,
gardens, lunchtime benches, the park air
chipped by cocky gossip, scuffed
with a cheap and streetwise chatter.
Drab, in that uniform brown utility
dubbed serviceable by an older generation
who shook tablecloths, leaving a scatter
of crumbs in backyards, or on kitchen steps.

So common they could slip, despite the Bible's words,
unnoticed, out of days too caught up with
the first swallow's forked flight, a cuckoo,
all the glittering indifference of spring.

Only as their society shrank, silent,
were they sudden news. Polished chestnut backs
counted for something. In ones and twos
they were watched over, their fat beaks tempted
into staying, sharing; valued
for their everyday reassurance, their gritty
resolution, their common-sense mirror of us,
their shabby survival tricks, their necessary lives.

School Photograph: 1957

Everything before them—playground, camera,
the man under the black hood in control.
Even Miss Turner does what she's told,
knowing how long a shade these photos cast.
The front row's cross-legged, white-socked, ruler-straight,
laughing, squinting at the sun, giggling *Cheese*,
fingering summer and its shadow edges
sharp as razors, and the grass shaved close, cut
and cut and cut all through the growing months:
bright with smiles and eaten up with curiosity,
not cancer. They've nothing to lose, except
play time, sitting here thick among friends,
how this will be for ever and ever,
always home with bread buttered, and cake
and food as innocent as skipping,
as safe as grace. They haven't invented
excuses, alibis, the cop-out clauses for doing well,
reasons for Valium, cloaks of diagnosis.
So busy being children they don't know
what children stretch into, how much or how long.
Shining, clenched into happy-ever-after,
here's how they sit before it all goes wrong.

Self-Portrait: With Camera

All exaggeration; nothing but sand,
flat as paper, and attenuated shadow
reaching up the print. Crane-fly
by Giacometti caught, monotone grey on grey,
an absurdity of angular sticks, yards high.
Racked torture. Semaphore elbows at head level,
pin scale: clutch of frenzy or camera,
but frenzy frozen out by shifting
sundown winds.

Only an outline, and that untrue:
weightless distortions, archetype of the faceless
and unidentifiable. Able to slip under doors,
watch from chiaroscuro galleries
and stalk the moon's phases; never on parade,
soluble at noon, but persistent, growing
more fluent towards dusk.

I call it my best likeness.

Red Interior: Still Life on a Blue Table

1947—the year when snow
blanking out colour, form, feature
became its own landmark—
Henri Matisse splurged a whole ration book
of red and blue.
Red walls, crazy with colour,
cracking with heat; tomatoes fat with sun,
spilling from the pool of a blue dish.

What is not red is blue is gold is green.

Three delphiniums
angle for air in a liquid vase,
and beyond the golden shutter a shaded green garden
throbs with loud summer,
greedy with living, its language
blazing this brilliant primary *yes*,
dazzled and hard-edged. It flames
with never knowing snow,
never being born into drifting whiteness,
not crying with milky cold
or slush-grey skies.

Instead, this red interior—
already grown up, confident of its own palette—
is steeped in sunlight, its bones
warm and supple as willow,
free with unlimited heat, its red
shouting through open windows to blue sky.

What Time is it, Mr Wolf?

Mr Wolf has eyes screwed tight, his fists
balled into dumplings, concentrating
on the rules. Today he's learned thistles,
a difficult door-handle, *excuse me*,
crackle of the cornflakes packet, the cat's nose,
broccoli, striped curtains, woodlice,
the smell of doormats. He has eaten
half a boiled egg, toast with Marmite
(but left the crusts), a banana.

The sun tickles like a blanket, the sort
his aunt keeps spare in a wheezing wardrobe
where sneezes hide. He knows
he mustn't laugh at the sun's fingers
but keep as still as church. He wants to feel
how they creep closer, mummy, daddy,
inching like grasshoppers, like the giggle
that can't be stoppered. He's got to get this right,
listening in puckered darkness
for the tilt of shadows,
for light splitting open,
for *Dinner time*!

If the Paper Bag can Learn to Fly—

and this is only the first lesson, working
from a self-help manual discarded
by one who'd already got the hang of it—
there'll be undreamed of opportunities.
This street is just a beginning.

Other streets will have tarmac pitted
in different patterns, or complex weather systems
round the gutters. *Waiting* and *No Waiting*
are warnings ready to be learned.
It's all one way, once you've mastered take-off.

Why lie here, flap-happy, when you can be active
translating the speeding, lit-up, narrow bends
around the corner? A fine place
to be a paper bag, free as air,
riding the up-draught in a slow glide.

It's still a question of *If*... and no answer
from whoever left this book behind,
pages ruffling in the slip-stream.

Spring

Sun draws a faint smile
from the winter branches
and soon, along the field edge,
every tree is laughing
loud and green and long.

Blackbird

He's landed on his feet, this one,
blinking in criss-cross frenzy of ants
fired up on hot stones. They run
zigzag, anyhow, freestyle; black slants
of panic, pepper-dust, while he's claw-deep
in tea-time, picking them off,
ripe as berries. He's hopping, squaring up,
landing new angles, straight in, trough-
eager, happy as Puck.
Just out of the nest, and can hardly believe his luck.

Not Even in Colour

What I didn't know then, but have learned to know now
is that the foreign films you took me to
weren't your own passion, but picked up.

I was still going to films for happy endings
like I read novels for stories, poems for rhyme
so I never understood your misty cravings
for the *Seven Samurai*, or Ingmar Bergman.

They weren't even in colour. After an evening
sitting in darkness watching different darkness
flickering in front of us, without the comfort of ice cream,
surrounded by serious and solitary silences,
it was back to your flat, hoping
you could tell me what we'd been looking at.
Something was significant, but why
did it have to be in a foreign language?
Reading the subtitles never helped.

And you could never explain your absences, the way
(although you'd seen each film before)
you couldn't remember names, who found true love,
or why no one got married. Sometimes
you even whispered me into someone else.

Black Swans, Mating

He, she, one neck crossing the other
caressing, a kiss of sable muscle,
and the surprise of their soft mew, mew;
sweet soprano at swim over the lake;
sipping, tasting for each other.
Soft as rain,
as dusk, their blacks mingling,
coiling and uncoiling, a silken knotting.
Storm clouds.
Then the slow, shallow slide,
he over her, sinking her
into the paddling waters, her head
up, her bill a flame, scarlet
and wide, wide, full throttle,
shrill in a sudden strangeness,
her foreign colour flooded, seeded,
and with the sheen of ebony.

Marriage Bed

She is stitching his love letters across
the honeymoon cotton of a double quilt
where the long sentences ride over their sleep.

Chain stitch. The looping line on line pricked deep
into weave still bearing the iron's bruise
with all the hot creases and pressed scars.

The knots are inside, bitten off—chewed
and illegible tracings of negative print.
This is the downside, read in the mirror.

Her hairs catch on pointed words,
text messages, tattoos, where the stab and thrust
pins them, homefast. She chooses red,

has bought more reels of carmine thread
than her suitcase can close on, and a fistful
of needles. A labour of love, curling

into the hooks and claws of question marks,
the scarlet punctuation he prefers.
No-one laughs at love, how it takes over,

how his words flow across the cotton.
She soaks her hands' meat in the salt
of commitment, ignoring the blood.

Familiars

They creep in darkness, moving
furniture back to lost positions

breathing by inches, licking
moonlight from loose slates

holding hands with mirrors, trailing
coded messages through wardrobes.

Silence goes unanswered, mouthing
spaces between curtains not quite closed

letting the locks creak, spiralling
through the eye of the needle

as the dead hours strike.

Muse

Go on, she says, arms folded,
hugging herself. *Give it a push.*
That devil-smile you feel inside your own
caught casually once in a photograph,
off-guard. *It'll run*, she says,
hunching complicit,
tucked into kitchen gossip. Close up
she could do with a wash,
and how she spent last night's
nobody's business. Her cigarette's
an unfamiliar brand, and unforgettable.
Go for it, she says. How
many other houses this morning,
kerb-crawling how many kitchens?
Never a borrower; sometimes months
between generous visits, between
one bony elbowing, and the next.
Prison, possibly, hints her grey
indoor pallor, or an affair gone
rough against the grain.
You'd never ask, or she'd be off
leaving smudged lipstick cheaply on her cup
before the real work starts. But she's done
enough. *Go on. Blame me.*

Clever Ways to Create a Clutter-Free Spacious Home

Identify the problem corners. You are not alone—
though that in itself is no encouragement.

That you have covered every wall—rag-rolled, silk,
or blood—only makes it harder.

Consider doors—and when, exactly,
you last used one. You have not yet escaped.

Be honest: every year you brought more stones
indoors as paperweights, or for their uselessness.

Windows open onto emptiness.
Reflect on this, without mirrors.

Discard all magazines; they only prescribe
ways you would never have considered reasonable.

These are the clever ways. The simple ones
are incalculably more difficult.

The Day after Valentine's Day

The streets are quiet. Not in the stretching
time-off way of Sunday mornings, or
the big-match-on-TV Saturday silence
or royal funeral hush, just

quiet. Empty quiet.
The nothing-to-say collapsed quiet
of the day after the event

when whatever was coming has gone
and being over is the only thing left.
Too grey for shadows or birdsong or leaves

and Sainsbury's which yesterday had hoped
for love in abundance, cuts its losses.
Armfuls of flowers only £1.

Nearly the Happy Hour

Sometimes arrives early, grabs a window table
and the waiter's eye. Orders Chardonnay

but Perhaps isn't sure she's ready yet
and wants more time with the menu

and Maybe is trying to remember
what she enjoyed last time.

Possibly, crushing her cigarette among the bent stubs,
asks *I wonder what's happened to Now*?

Morning Milk

You say
I have perfected ways of opening a milk carton
and for this reason you will stay with me.

You admire
its wings, clean lines for flight.
A natural balance, like a butterfly.

You remember
the clouded bottles set on proud front steps,
chill sentinels to school. Their familiar sourness.

You talk
of morning crates, clattering at the run.
Lateness; how cold September mornings are.

Owls

The thunder's still far off, bickering
over the next county's fresh stubble, but

closer, a couple of owls, tawnies, bantering
across dry gardens, pines apart,

their *tsk tsk* unfamiliar, countering
school-book stereotypes, split

sleep from its darkness, lighting
the night's long heat, hot slates, until

dropping in, between the chimneys, sidling
along the roofline, side by side

and up on the tiles, they're edging into sex,
the whole restless city willing them on.

Late Valencias

Before I open my eyes you have squeezed
these best of oranges
into my favourite glass.

You do this to remind me of our train
threading through gloss-green orange groves
out of Seville to sleepy Cordoba

or that time in the Real Alcazar
when stubborn fruit and blossom clung together
in limp November

or how we felt their scented heat
among the Holy Week processions, winding
the crowded nights with hoods and candles.

This house

loves summer, loves
doors all-day stretching to hot lawns, loves
yawning windows, loves
slow hammock-swing of curtains, loves
spiralling child-pitch of voices, loves
hay-smells and pollen, loves
its cool and shadowed kitchen, loves
lemons and cucumbers, garden berries, loves
crack of heat in its joists, loves
arthritic easings, creak of wooden weight, loves
shuttered corners with the lazy buzz of bees, loves
the calendar of visits, loves
lavender and butterflies, loves
itself.

Hugo

What he remembers of us is *Dolls, dolls*!
leaping to hold them; here his smile
is cracking five-years wide, lighting
with sunburst adoration for
the fat matroyshka's face and flowered ball.
She splits her belly, opens up, to show
her smaller, slimmer twin. *Again*!
Again!—shouts clap to greet each one,
each smiling mother popping from the cup
he's tugged and wrestled into birth.
He counts and grins and lines them. Ten, in all.
All thumbs, he sheathes them back
in ordered hide and seek, until
all's one. Again. All done.

Tell him they're Russian, from St Petersburg,
bought under dirty amber lights, where nights
of nicotine had tarred the walls,
where cities change their names to hide
a history, and he'll just smile.
It's not his story, yet. He wants, again,
to unwrap these sunlit generations, daughter
after daughter: their storyless and tidy fit
gives satisfying comfort. Even now
he understands enough of families to know
the smallest gets the most protection, and outside—
friends, far and near relations, playmates, loves—
somehow, we all fit in.

Cormorants

Out there, a sandbar black with solid sound
screaming a goal for the home team,
the fans gone wild, winging their *yah-yah-yah*
on every wave.
They're clamouring
for air, sea, space, fish—the clan,
a cormorant wall of outstretched wings
shaking their feathers free of the silky bay,
this couple of hundred supporters, beaks
yelling wide, *Come-on-on-on*.
And the tide
rolling in time, splashing their cries
across an estuary of eels and dabs,
their rough incessant rise and dive,
scrawling equations in a restless sea.

Today the winning formula brings them down,
webbed and sure-footed, cheering, insisting:
hurrahs gleaming like liquorice, a wet
and glistening chorus of success.

Attachments

You don't have to open them. It's enough
going back, just to check. They'll wait,
stuffed with a woodshedful of scraps.
Things that might have come in useful.

Or if you have an attic, like
living in a children's story, they'll be there—
boxes never unpacked from the last move,
with cuttings, snapshots, jaundiced newsprint.

Only you can decode them, pressing keys
to unlock time's encryption, explaining
their connections. If someone you love
understands just a small part, it's enough.

Hope

But the greatest of these…
Hope bit her lip,
glanced sideways at the competition line.

Faith sat serene, dreaming an inner trip
while Charity's complexion gave no sign
that she was being judged. The judge droned on:

how kind she was; not puffed up; well-behaved.
Hope chewed a nail, knowing the end foregone.
The cheering crowd threw up balloons and waved.

…is Charity.
Of course it was. Faith blinked,
shaken at last. The spotlight sought its prey.

What are your interests, love? Charity winked:
people, small children, animals; the way
to every heart. So pure and simple, yet

she blossomed on the public stage. No fear,
no trembling shyness. Hope, with cigarette,
veiled her sour scowls with smoke. She'd win. Next year.

Swans

We took to feeding the swans for good luck
after chain store orders dried up, shackling the machines.
Something to do, with our hands; *not used*
to idleness, Sharon said
twisting her rings, tearing damp bread into strips,
like the lint Ron used oiling the overlocker.
It helps. Takes your mind off. Gives you something.

Only two at first, drifting past as if
they hadn't meant to be there. Perhaps they wanted
a lake hung with willows, honeysuckle, a distant cuckoo.
Calendar land. Not our canal—
our coffee-coloured swillage, downside waste
of beer bottles, coke cans, smudging papers
dissolving half-afloat beside the tow path.
Mick said they were lost. But didn't look it.
Missionaries, Neema said. Their whiteness.
And laughed into her cigarette. It was Sharon
threw them the bread, liking their hose necks
nuzzling for it. Afterwards, she said,
she felt lighter, like flying, some
of their cleanness rubbing off. Flew,
with a pocketful of bright ideas.

Then two more. Annie shared her lunch,
collected their down, made a wedding cape,
and a christening shawl with the remnants.
Ron picked a feather, quilled words into a book
best-selling the world. Lee brought them seed,
copied their nests, built himself a farm.

Every day more and more. The canal
was light with them; we cleared the condoms,
lottery tickets, pizza vouchers; planted grasses, deodars,
a magnolia tall as a church. Anita sang
her childhood, spun it as a golden disc.
The financial pages asked us for tips, listened
when we said nothing they'd heard before.
Dave took down their histories, their water ways,
created a School within the University.

A bishop came for blessing. Swamis, seers
shuffled in barefoot lines to stroke their presence.
A stammer, smoothed like a mirror, spoke of healing,
and a severed hand rejoined its mourning nerves.
Sheila made icons, gave them to the sick,
and someone whispered *miracles*.

We'd our hands full, stitching this together.
The machines sang overtime—sheets, saris,
sixty styles of shirt, a train sewn
                                        with embroidered snowdrops.
The silky scarf of swan's breath we sent to Sharon
for every day, drawing her back,
needing her strong hands: to read our luck's small print,
to feed the swans,
to understand.

Calling Up

Hooked on the earpiece, she hears the house ring,
hears hall tiles, cracked crazy as laughter,
doormat's mousy creep, a coat peg's feisty thrust.
There's the newel, old bruiser, swinging in,
always a satchel hanging, the dog's lead,
a shred of wallpaper curling.
She fingers on the dresser a clutch of gloves,
cards for posting, bills, cat fur
behind the plates. Hears circling goldfish,
a pile of newspapers settling their arguments;
hangs on for company, the bell voices
ringing to each other, bouncing off
skewed steps to the garden, doors, spaces beyond.
She hears the house ring, house ring,
house ring.
Not answering.

Keeping in Touch

She crams each page like a mad woman,
hugs every margin, scared of space
where doubts and contradictions seed
like weeds. And capitals!
Loves them: slams them loud
among lurching words, their jagged heads
up, up above the parapets.

Not an inch unused; even her address
cropped short, last week's date
shouldered off the page.
Her fingers race. She packs ragged questions
into corners, shoving past today
to prise open cupboard doors,
shuffle the thumbed and faded photographs.

She's shouting across hundreds of miles
her ink blotchy with loneliness,
noisy with need, her hands on shared past
and her arms arching wide through the letter box.

Seen from the Train

High speed rattle, and you could have missed her,
glancing out, thinking a hundred miles ahead,
next week, or Christmas. A blink.
But you didn't. A bridge—right?—
and you go under, so
you see her both sides, standing, a car
pulled over, the road a lumpy tarmac
linking somewhere to somewhere else.
Look back, as the train puts on distance,
and there's her phone, left side.
No face. Her hair was—what? Already
you've had Hopper in, making her flat as paint,
colouring the unremembered: a sheen
that could have been rain, a leather jacket,
the fields emptied for winter.
Perhaps it wasn't a phone.

Cross-examined,
giving the only evidence,
you're a poor witness.

Red

Not even the faintest mark on the calendar, yet
the day throbs, pulsing
with purpose. It's lined up, in the sights,
all its routes mapped out. A day
gliding smoothly up on impressive tyres,
right on target. All the precision
of an oiled gun.

This is the day they'll always remember—
where they were, the weather,
how the pavements looked, how the sky
angled and tipped and buckled.
Make it red. *Red.*

Taking the Photo

The first camera she can lay her hands on—
not even digital, just the light-weight
holiday snapper we took to Venice—
and her fingers determined not to tremble.
Take my photo, she says, not smiling,
her eyes clouding in their crystal. *Now,*
as I am—as if laughing
on Torcello or haloed in pigeon-blur
clutching the map of St Mark's
is no longer her likeness.
Warts and all, she says. For the first time I see
the hairline wrinkles and small change paid over
against time. *The photo you'll have to take*—
her voice has emptied certainty out like
a heap of sand—*round the streets, the hospitals,*
the web, the newspapers. Asking. Afterwards.
When it's happened.

Her eyes return.

And then I'll take yours.

Cooking on the Car Radio

calls down saddle of hare, slapping it
under wipers, flick of salt, screen wash

and slip a knife up the long bone, like this

past sealed, shuttered lorries, secret
as chocolate bars

remember
to catch the blood, a basin or a jug

verges, grey with salt: too-long winter
cocooned in steel, spinning out the wheels

with onions, or preferably shallots

making sense of maps, where slip-roads slither in,
watching brake lights, blink of intentions

do this quickly before the fat congeals

wondering on the by-pass why floured hands
are kneading dumplings in the dashboard,
chopping herbs in a lay-by; stink of diesel

and some juniper berries. Top of the oven

through the heater; road well-greased, black
as burned meat tins.

Gull

You cannot look away. You cannot tear your eyes
from muscular percussion, from the hammering
down down down of his bill. You might take in
those webbed pink feet anchoring his weight,
that back of gleaming steel, his broad chest
feathered salt-white, how he works from the neck.
You might recall this, afterwards.
But now, precision: the piercing smash
of crab-shell on stone, the splay of claws,
how each blow splinters more, more tough casing,
how he concentrates to scatter
all the life out, to shatter useless armour.
You hope the children look away—they might
be storing it up for nightmares
like television news. You hope he's not their gull
who swooped for fish and chips, whose *ka-ka*-calling
woke you at six to watch black fishing boats
slide down grey shingle into the sun's eye.
Now it's too late not to know how killing feels,
how each crash drives this yellow bill deeper,
pounding pounding pounding. Later,
you might remember the estuary mud, its slow plopping,
the mesh and flow of seeping rivulets, a backdrop
familiar as summer. And how you recognised
his beak's scarlet spot *in out in out*,
and greed
drawing you down.

Undoing Time

It was so simple. Slipping the hands
in secret he launched a whole shipwreck
of schemes, just by altering the clocks.

Stealing back twenty minutes took the check
off order, let time, unanchored, drift
on lazier tides, towards uncharted rocks.

Arrangements sanctioned by his shift
of policy foundered on the sands
in bays of submerged seconds: off-course

they were flotsam, their mechanical tick-tock-tick
no longer countered. All at once the force
of time was nothing, just a gentle grip

his frail wrists could dissolve. He'd thought the ship
of life a sober, decent cruise; no slick
to foul its passage, a discipline too pure

to yield to sabotage. But once he'd learned the trick
of slackening the cables, he was sure
he could untie the whole day's careful moorings,
leaving its raft of plans unhitched and insecure.

Shoes

With no one left to argue with
the bags fill up, splitting a life
between the council tip and charity shop.

It's almost easy, emptying his shirts,
the one good suit. There's rhythm in
thin skeleton hangers rattling on the rail.

Moving. Moving on, like they said.
Giving the cupboards back their breathing space
and elbow room and arms length.

And then there are the shoes.
Obedient, she ties the laces, knots them tight,
in pairs. In pairs. Just like they said.

Sleep

I never really noticed sleep when it came
floating like plump cumulus
after a summer day and everything stretched out right.

It just happened, in the way
the next breath arrives, or the heart beats,
or the problem, slept on, always has a solution.

It fitted simply into a patchwork
of day and night, nothing rare
or remarkable in its unassuming habits

so I never really noticed how
we never talked about it, taking it for granted,
like eternal youth, and being happy ever after.

We never whispered, watchful, as
nervous of a stranger, or someone
we needed to win favour from

or as in that foreign country
where language overturns all the rules,
then shrugs and walks away.

Handkerchiefs

She wants to remember, but it's years
since she had a proper handkerchief,
one that could carry a knot.

A clean one every day to school,
shaking out squares as regular
as four times table, its everyday print
fading. Then her first ironing,
learning folds before she knew fractions.
The Christmas presentation boxes
pinned and fanned like peacocks' tails,
her curled initials embroidered, flowering.
Lace corners for best. Her mother's careful
grading of handkerchiefs, and days,
and fresh air gulped from their centres
in the playground misery of crying, and growing up
through weddings and funerals
                                        and somewhere in between
the children. The children. And now
there's only these boxes of paper, all throw-away.

Nothing to knot,
and what she wanted to remember gone.
She can't remember anything. Except the handkerchiefs.

Late October

Time fattens in slack sunlight. On the ground
weak shadows blend and blur. A breeze weaves
endless music in slow strokes: the sound
of leaves falling through leaves falling through leaves.

Absence

The day she died a neighbour worked all day
pruning his apple trees. With slow snip-snip
he nosed the surgeon secateurs to strip
exhausted, over-crowded wood away.

December drizzle drifted from the grey
irrelevant clouds, and sounds merged. Here the chip
and chink of endless tea-cups; there the slip
of branch on branch, falling on sodden clay.

Due labours for that month. A colander
held windfall apples, shrivelling, scarred and brown
around each bruise. A yellowed calendar
(*Seeds and Farm Sundries*) now redundant, swung
askew beside where her old raincoat hung
which no-one, yet, could speak of taking down.

Windfalls

Bruised, and with badges of their rottenness,
the wasps' wreckage and drunken leavings,
they line up by the sink.
Apples, pears, skins that held plums—
nursery pictures. Each day
I bring them in, their sweet decay
spicing this kitchen, coaxing a long evening
of simmering and straining, a hoard against winter,
and nothing wasted.

I recall my mother, grateful for such fruit,
her careful rescuing of what was good: her work.

Choose her old knife
its blade still scooped to sharpness
and begin.

Spice Jars

They stood for years, high on the pantry shelf.
Then dust to dust: loose stoppers, grey and furred,
greasy with age, neglect, the labels blurred,
each spice surrendering its ancient self
turned pensioner-apologetic, yet
leaving a perfect circle clean when lifted
like some domestic chess piece shifted
in one last game, or stately minuet.

I opened one: faint kitchen scents (a trace
of fruit breads, Welsh cakes, and the kitchen warm
and welcoming from school) took shadow form:
allspice and nutmeg, cinnamon and mace,
caraway for seed cakes or for loaves,
and dry, black-budded rattlings of cloves.

Coats

Then there's the one for dead of winter,
the funeral coat, that doesn't hang
among the walking jackets for weekends
or the weekday raincoats,
but breathes the silence of the wardrobe.

Never in fashion, its must-have
came from need, out of that first
black urgency, prescribing
how all the later funerals would be dressed.

It was never comfortable (too tight
around the neck) and now
it's fitting closer. There's less give
across the shoulders, and the hem
has thickened

and after all the crumpled salt of old tissues
its pockets are never empty.

White Out

In the silence after the engine stops
snow prints a map of the world across
the windscreen's lectern. Under this jigsaw
of sliding continents, of drift, the slew
of invisible currents tracking fault lines,
lies a cloudscape of breath.

Every winter the radio leaks stories—
what happens, how slowly, what to carry
in case of emergency. Such a night
as this, sightless, unlooked for,
hushed. Perhaps the jigsaw is complete at last.
Intended, even. But the door still opens, hard
on a reassuringly imperfect white.

Winter Habits

He reads his e-mail, watching her
filling a hot-water bottle, folding
the neck for safety, as her mother did.
In the chimney the wind repeats
loud winter verses, and the lights
flicker. He thinks of candles
stored deep inside the dresser drawers
against emergencies, and wonders
if she would think to place each one before a mirror,
doubling the light. Her mother did,
and had the saving habit—string,
emptied cotton reels, odd buttons, tins—
things which might come in useful.

Winter brings out the old in us, he thinks,
familiar peasant ways; and clicks
to mail his message, wondering
who now hoards jam jars, or hems handkerchiefs.

Prospect

Each generation, the ones who took the last, like gods,
claim that the ore's worked out. They say
they pity you: only this worthless rock
to drudge at; that they had the best of it,
as of everything; that they don't envy you.
So many have been here before.

You listen, hearing the unmapped waters tell you
how its beginnings are still new, how the earth
never spends all its secrets. In the stream
you see a glint, a glimmer,
the teasing glitter.
Here you will dip the water, pan for gold.

High Flight

By chance, a jet high-flying chalks
a line angled over three century-old Scots pines
under a level bank of cloud at 45°
to a slab of cumulus, providing
an empty triangle of sky.

Only for a moment. The chalk line shifts,
slipping behind the pines. Geometry
slumps into falling haze
and a feathered, breathed out, blurring line
like white dust memories of maths.

It's not proofs that remain, but how
our rough books were pink, fat and fuzzed
around the edges; how we had to show
working out, something you got marks for,
even if the ending came out wrong—

although later this was never
how it happened. Now you get there any way you can—
bending the rules, watching them
break up behind you, breathless
and unstable as the reckoning of clouds.

The Going-Away Dress

Now it's the only one left in the wardrobe
slanted sideways on the tarnished rail, looking
over its shoulder, swinging
on a padded sateen hanger.

Still not out of fashion, though seasons
of going are always changing—baby,
bridal, through all the shades of fading
into one colour, any colour, the only colour.

It wears itself lightly, this dress—floating
on butterflies, closed wings praying.
Always the perfect fit, ready to slip
so easy from its perch; this year, next year,

sometime. It sighs like silk
inhaling the dust of its own passport.
A dress for departing on a single ticket,
with a bag of bruised apples, half a loaf.

It could be night. Or autumn. Or soon.
Sometimes you can hear its half-creak,
this side of ghostly, straining for the date
of release; the brilliant daylight; away.

One Last Thing

They'll only laugh, clucking round his pillows
at this one thing left unfinished,
the one last thing. Already
beyond the sterile double glazing
there are willows scribbled green,
and the grass is stubble, has an itch
for growing, along with coltsfoot
gangly in the corners and celandines
opening gold. If he could walk
he'd walk north with them, keeping step
with spring, two miles an hour, pushing
up country, over motorways, across car parks,
landfill; past people living lives screened,
curtained, watched, confined; beyond towns
burning all night with lights, through squares
stiff with the statues of dead aldermen.
He'd cross out everything from all the lists,
leave only this: two miles an hour,
hearing leaves open as he passed,
a snap of buds; breathing.

The Other Side

Small things, at first. Nothing beyond
sunlight pouring through you, dazzling,
as a dog turns to bark, puzzling its owner.
The bus roars past, despite your outstretched arm.

Shop assistants still gossip across you,
telling last night over and over, while you miss
your reflection in mirrors or windows
and the shadow tied to your heels.

When you turn the tap, washing your finger prints,
cold water swirls like fog, like a draught of air.
Then doors only half ajar;
a cat's width. A crack.

Stairs keep their silences; no creak
when you walk the landing, where tall moonlight
holds its ruled edges. And, at last,

all the freedom you ever wanted.